MW00460507

Life WITH(OUT) KIRK

A broken path that finds direction

David Coleman
with Peter Lundell

To Kirk's dad, Cody

From one father to another

ACKNOWLEDGEMENTS

I often hear people say " I can't thank them enough". I certainly, without a doubt, know that this applies to Mr. Lundell. He is Professional and Knowledgeable. He was so Caring and Compassionate. He was so subtle with his approach to letting me know when my thoughts "went rouge", the email would read " David, what would you like me to do with this paragraph"? "This ideology seems kinda odd"? Many, many hours on the phone with me, and even with my wife, to make sure our thoughts were understood. I was so fortunate for having the opportunity to personally meet Peter and his beautiful wife.

Thank you Mr. Lundell.
Blessings

CONTENTS

Chapter 1
Ways Things Should Have Been..1

Chapter 2
This Is Not Happening...5

Chapter 3
Facing What We Don't Want To See..12

Chapter 4
When Truth Is Worse than Lies...20

Chapter 5
Hoping for Justice..26

Chapter 6
Kirk's Law—a Blessing from Tragedy..32

Chapter 7
Closure Eludes Us...38

Chapter 8
Finding Faith...45

Chapter 9
Closure Arrives...53

Chapter 10
Darkness to Light...60

Chapter 11
Stumbling Toward Hope...68

Chapter 12
Seeing Past the Pain...74

I THINK WE ALL could admit to having been led down a broken path. And I am thankful for the people who provided me guidance in seeking direction. The storms are still present, but the way I weather through them has changed. Knowing I have a source of strength, worthy of honor and glory, now lessens them to a mere sprinkle, allowing me to skip through the puddles.

I love listening to music, and I had a collection of 120 cassette tapes and a vintage car cassette deck with a stereo system loud enough to make my ears bleed. Classic Rock will always hold a special place in my heart. Christian Contemporary / Christian Rock is now my music passion and an inspiration to gather my thoughts. I tell my story, acknowledging those artists and their songs that reached my searching soul.

Two sets of song lyrics express my heart in why I tell my story and how I have felt.

Well, everybody's got a story to tell
And everybody's got a wound to be healed

–Plumb[1]

To everyone who's lost someone they love
Long before it was their time
You feel like the days you had were not enough
When you said goodbye

–Third Day[2]

---

[1] Plumb, "Need You Now," on *Need You Now*. Curb, 2014.

[2] Third Day, "Cry Out To Jesus," on *Wherever You Are*. Essential Records, 2005.

CHAPTER 1

Ways Things Should Have Been

NINETEEN MONTHS. FOR SOME things in life, that's a long time. For a person's entire life, nineteen months is absurdly short.

How can you live your whole life in nineteen months? How can you enjoy a happy childhood, go to school, play ball, fall in love, do something crazy and different, get a job, marry, have kids, do your part to make the world a better place, and someday hold your grandchildren on your lap—all in nineteen months?

That's all the time Kirk was given.

I try to reason or explain or even comprehend how Kirk's life on earth could be so incredibly short.

How could all those years after the first nineteen months have been taken from him?

Even harder is knowing that I only spent a handful of times with such a wonderful gift, my grandson. I wish I could go back and re-schedule the opportunities I overlooked.

I wish I could re-do so many things.

•

I messed up from the start.

When Kirk was born on March 17, 2013, I was five hundred miles away at a very important event in Bristol, Tennessee—NASCAR racing. During the race my son Cody called with the big news, Kirk Antonio Coleman had successfully entered this world. I was so happy for him. And so disappointed for not being there with him.

When I told Cody I was sorry not to be there, he was as understanding and forgiving as a racing enthusiast could be when he said, "But Dad, it's Bristol!" Cody and his brother Chad had been to lots of racetracks, both NASCAR and local tracks, but Bristol was our favorite.

Yet today I don't remember who won the race.

What I remember is that a child was born.

The excitement in Cody's voice was the same that I experienced as a dad when he and his two brothers were born. If you haven't experienced it for yourself, those are the proudest moments in a parent's life, just ask any parent—or at least a dad. Poor Mom is recovering from it all. This time, Anissa, baby Kirk's mother, was recovering well.

That happy, healthy kind of pride is just as strong when your grandchildren are born. And because Grandma doesn't have to recover this time, she can feel it too.

•

My son was well on his way to manhood, or so it seemed. He found the girl of his dreams, and now that she was with child, I got to help them move into their first apartment together. But just like his father, isn't there supposed to be a wedding first? I have tried to always be supportive of all my children; I also let them know my feelings on major life choices. But just like my management training—hard on issues, soft on people. I liked Anissa. They had met in high school, and she was good for Cody. They were the cutest couple with the cutest little boy. My son made my heart warm, and Anissa and Kirk added to that warmth.

But my dreams for them didn't find their way to reality. Sadly, for their reasons they split up, and Anissa went to live with her parents, Tony and Angie Garza, along with her sister Anndrea. Thankfully, Cody and Anissa remained kind to each other, and he often went there for dinner and spent the evening with the Garzas. Like Cody, Anissa was so young and needed her parents' and sister's help in taking care of Kirk.

But despite whatever happened, Kirk wanted for nothing. He was very loved. A happy baby.

•

We sometimes wondered what kind of man Kirk would become because as a baby he never crawled. Crawling is what babies do, or are supposed to do. Not Kirk. He would extend one foot and then the other and pull himself forward with knuckles on the floor—call it a monkey scoot. He could move clear across any room, fast. Then in a single day he went from the monkey scoot to standing up.

When he came to visit my wife, Karrie, and me, he got busy. He would go to Karrie's potted plants and shove his hands into the dirt. He'd wriggle his hands in the soil, squeeze the dirt, then throw it on the floor. Try as we did, we couldn't keep him away from the plants.

When he ate food in his high chair, he'd throw pieces of his hot dog on the floor. He wanted to feed the dog.

Then he'd throw his sippy cup on the floor.—"Don't do that again, Kirk."—Then he'd do it again. It was fun, of course, and necessitated repetition.

He was always entertaining. Sometimes the feeling was *Augh!* But he was so cute that we could never get mad.

We only wished we could have spent more time with him. But we all had jobs. We were all busy. Every day. And if we didn't have time to spend with Kirk, we'd always have time later. So we thought.

CHAPTER 2

This Is Not Happening

CODY CALLED AGAIN ON October 29, 2014.

Again I was away, this time vacationing in Florida with Karrie and her father, one thousand, three hundred miles away.

Two days earlier Karrie and I had searched the gift shops for trinkets to bring back for our grandsons. We found a keychain with "Hunter" on it. That was good for our two-year-old grandson, son of Chad, Cody's older brother. But no "Kirk," was to be found in the *K* section. Then a fitting substitute, "Little Monster," meant affectionately of course, was perfect for little Kirk, who was, as I often said, "all boy and full of spirit."

The morning of the day Cody called, Karrie and I walked under the palm trees along the beach of Marco Island. We enjoyed the morning sun and surf as we collected seashells—a perfect day, worthy of a vacation calendar.

Our perfect day continued as we sat we sat poolside after our walk. Lunchtime arrived, so we decided to go make a couple of sandwiches. I picked up my phone that been sitting beside me, set to vibrate and unheard amid the pool noises.

Missed calls. Same with my wife's phone. Missed calls.

Multiple missed calls from Cody and from Anissa.

Those two were always breaking up and getting back together, so I thought maybe they wanted to talk about something or tell us how they were.

I called him back.

"Dad . . . he's gone." Cody choked up. "Kirk's gone."

WHAT? I could not be hearing this. Cody did not say that. It could not be.

Cody was silent.

"No. . . . No." I said.

Maybe Kirk wandered off and got lost. But I knew that's not what Cody meant.

What on earth could have happened?

Silence on the other end. Did the phone get cut off? No. Still there.

"How did this happen?"

"He choked."

"Choked? How does a nineteen-month-old little boy choke?

Cody said nothing.

"Choked on what?"

He did not respond.

"How could such a thing even be possible?"

Silence.

Wait. What am I doing? Quit asking questions, Dave! I need to be sympathetic. My son needs me now more than ever.

Another voice came over the phone, Angie, Anissa's mother. "She did everything she could."

Those were her first words. I waited for more.

"She got him to take a couple of breaths, and then she lost him."

"What happened?"

"Kirk stopped breathing. He was choking."

"Choking on what?"

"Eggs. They were eating eggs."

"Where?"

"At the babysitter's." Angie paused and took a deep breath. "She had EMT training."

Really?

"She had him breathing again for a few short breaths, but couldn't save him."

No way.

This did not happen.

And I was not hearing it.

But it did, and I was.

"She did everything she could."

And I unwillingly accepted that God allowed Kirk to go to heaven this day.

•

I was beside myself, feeling helpless and devastated.

Karrie and I were so shocked that the baby sitter was an EMT, and yet she couldn't save Kirk.

Kids choke on toys. But eggs?

Answers. I needed answers.

And we needed to get home. Now.

A phone call to the airline resulted in, "We can't change your flight from Saturday to today." It was Wednesday. My father-in-law drove us on an hour-long, silent trip to the airport. Upon arrival we dashed from ticket counter to ticket counter. "When is the soonest flight to Chicago?" We eventually bought two tickets on a flight departing in a couple of hours. Since we purchased the tickets so close to takeoff time, my wife and I couldn't get seats together. It was the longest three hours of misery I have ever experienced. All I could do the whole flight was stare at a picture of Kirk on my phone and fight back the tears.

I sat in a middle seat, and the guys on either side of me were probably miserable too, wondering the whole time what on earth was wrong with this man sitting between them, staring at a photo of a baby boy and trying to hide the obvious fact that he was crying the whole time.

My brother Kim and his wife picked us up at O'Hare. Another long ride, this time in the dark with a few things said about Kirk and mostly emotionally broken silence, until we stumbled into our house at 1 a.m. We didn't sleep much at all.

The next morning I sat in my recliner chair all the way back. I stared at the same photo of Kirk on my phone.

I wished I could disappear.

"You need to get up and take a shower," Karrie said.

"Why?"

"We're meeting Anissa's family. That's why."

"I just want to sit here."

"And you need to eat."

I sat there until she dragged me.

•

Cody showed up at our house, along with my ex-wife, who brought our other grandson, Hunter.

We drove together to grandmother Angie's house, where daughter Anissa lived with Kirk. Lots of family members had already gathered there and formed a genuine crowd.

Their otherwise lovely house felt heavy and dark, and an utter sadness hung in the air like a fog. Everyone was talking, sitting around, trying to put all the pieces together, and support Anissa and Cody and her parents and each other in everyone's shared shock and brokenness.

Hunter was two and a half, ten months older than Kirk, and he wanted to play. We told him that his cousin had gone to heaven, and his two-year-old mind figured, *Okay. That's a good place. I want to ride his car.*

From Disney's *Cars* movie Kirk had a motorized, battery-operated tow truck in the form of the character Mater, the rusty tow truck. Hunter wanted to ride in it—"No, Hunter"—"Yes!"—"No!"—"Why not?"

It was Kirk's toy. And it had now taken on an air of sacredness that could not longer be touched.

Hunter could only feel his two-year-old's sense of indignation.

Then he moved toward the fireplace for more opportunity. Next to it Kirk's panoply of toys were all neatly stacked. Cars, trucks, and monkey toys. Lots of monkeys. Anissa loved monkeys. And Hunter wanted to play—"No, Hunter! Not now"—"Harrumph!"

Anissa's grandfather was a deacon at a church where he had a friend who owned a funeral home, so with them the Garza family planned the whole funeral. My ex wasn't happy about being left out, but to me it was the best thing that could have happened.

When we left, all we did was hug and cry.

•

Back home, with the arrangements in place and the viewing two days away, I again became a recluse and retreated to my recliner, phone in hand, with Kirk's picture full screen. I stared at it, and I wondered about all the things I couldn't fathom.

The next day was to be the celebration of the fifty-second anniversary of my birth. But this time there would be no cake and no candles.

My emotions on fire, I didn't feel I had enough strength to go through with the coming days. I texted my oldest sister: *I can't do this!* I was in tears, a wreck, broken beyond words. She texted back, *I know you are stronger than you think.*

Even though I was the younger brother, she had always confided in me when she struggled. When she did, I detached my emotions and used my business training to help her through her situations. But doing that for myself—now—was an insurmountable task. Family and friends help get a person through the toughest times. Looking back, God gave me the strength. I realize that now.

I took my sister's words of encouragement with me as I slept but didn't sleep.

CHAPTER 3

Facing What We Don't Want To See

INSTEAD OF A BIRTHDAY cake, the next day arrived with an invitation to go skeet shooting with my three sons at a family friend's farm. It was an unseasonably warm and sunny November day in northern Indiana. And I hadn't held a gun since my Boy Scout days. One son pitched up skeets as another took aim. After each boy successfully hit a few of these moving targets, the shotgun was placed in my hands. Up went the clay pigeon, I took aim and fired— direct hit! If I were a smart man, I would have quit right then. But the pigeons were safe after that, at least from me, because I missed every one thereafter. But hit or miss, shooting at things was therapeutic and took my mind off the reality looming back home.

That evening, As much as I would have loved to keep the memories of the day's activities with my sons in my head until sleep overtook me, the dreaded thoughts of the next day's viewing crept into my head. Firmly planted in the recliner, I realized I needed help. It was getting late, and my wife was asleep in the next room. Should I wake her? The last days had taken their toll on us both. I let her sleep.

So of course I thought of Jim. He was one person whom I could call in the middle of the night and know would always be there for me. He was a man I admired greatly and felt proud to call my friend, one who would gladly come if I called. I remembered back to how we'd met.

My brother and I dabbled in different cars at our hometown racetrack, which was a dirt surface. After it closed down, we traveled to the next closest track, which was asphalt. There is much debate between dirt and asphalt race drivers, and not many can adapt to both surfaces with success at both. Most dirt racers hold the philosophy that "dirt is for racing, pavement is for getting there." Asphalt racers say that "dirt is for farming."

We once stripped down and pieced together a Mercury Bobcat, purchased from a co-worker for a hundred dollars. A racer friend who was a welder said he didn't want see anyone get hurt, so welded in the safety cage for us—such is the camaraderie within competitive racing. After many battle scars, a.k.a. dents, we got third place in season points and rookie of the year honors. The racing "bug" can be described as being like a gambling addiction, so with this limited success we traded our battered Bobcat for two undeveloped cars to build a title-contending car.

But shortly after we did, I was approached by a gentleman named Jim, who was interested in the Bobcat and explained that his five-year-old son would get more enjoyment out of playing in my old racer than on a new swing set. It turned out that his boy was my biggest fan. I was intrigued with Jim's philosophy on toys for his son and amazed that as a high school dropout, he knew more about fixing and building racecars then I could have imagined. I wish I had sold *him* the Bobcat.

Jim often worked late into the night, building stock racing cars out of pieces and parts from junkyards all over northern Indiana and southern Michigan.

Jim built some of the fastest racecars in this area, and as an amateur racecar driver, I was proud to have been able to drive them. I only wish I could have won more races for him because he was a hero to me both for the amazing cars he built and for the deep compassion he had toward me as well as our whole racing team.

Why am I thinking about all this stuff at a time like this? Of course it was to distract myself from otherwise fixating on Kirk's photo.

So should I call Jim? I finally concluded that simply knowing he would answer, listen, encourage—and even come if I asked—was comforting enough for me.

I wish that everyone had someone like Jim in their life.

•

At Kirk's viewing, the little guy lay in a child-sized casket. There should be no such thing as child-sized caskets because children shouldn't die. But they do.

No surprise, they had him wearing a little sweater with a monkey on it.

Looking at his tousled tan hair, long eyelashes, and little upturned nose, I couldn't help but imagine his opening those big, round, brown eyes and smiling, then rising up in a miracle—the way someone might fantasize or hope for a loved one. But he didn't.

And then the longer I looked at him, the less he looked like Kirk. Something wasn't right. He looked more like an imitation of

Kirk. Makeup. That was it. His face was thickly covered with coroner's makeup. And the funeral home employees monitored the casket and asked us all not to touch Kirk's face because it would distort the makeup.

So why did they go and put all that makeup on him in the first place? *Sheesh!*

I moved on—partly because it bothered me to see him like that and partly because so many people were crowding around. Anissa's parents both worked at a big RV manufacturer, and many of the employees were there. The Garza's were a very socially connected family.

It was no surprise when a young, tall, dark-haired man approached me. We knew each other because he and his brother often assisted the safety crew at the racetrack. He was also acquainted with Anissa's family, who often attended the races.

What did surprise me was that this friend wanted to know if we could visit his mother. He said that since Kirk's death, she had been depressed and hadn't left the house. So he thought it would be helpful for us to visit her. Strange, I didn't even know his mother. I assumed Anissa did. And why would he ask me here at the viewing? Well, though I'd never met her before, okay, I was willing to go.

Anissa said she would set a time with me and get back with them to arrange the visit.

But the visit never happened.

If it had, I wonder how it might have gone. How would the mother have responded? Did she even want us to visit? Or was it just her son's wanting us to go without her knowledge? I'll never know the answers to those questions, and as things would turn out, I didn't want to know.

Jim and his lovely wife, Beth Ann, were there. They came early, and their very presence took a huge weight off of me because I was dreading this day. Otherwise, I would have wished I could have brought my recliner, plopped it in a corner, and sat in it the whole time. But with Jim beside me I needed no recliner.

Also visiting were coworkers, including Homero, whose reaction when he saw little Kirk's lifeless body in that casket will be etched in my memory forever. Homero broke into tears and put his hand on my shoulder. "Dave, he's so small."

In that moment I struggled terribly to grasp even a glimpse of why God had allowed our little boy to die. Homero has a huge heart, big enough to share my pain that day—and I'm grateful he did.

After the viewing we came straight home.

Is this really happening? Why God?[3] Why do our loved ones have to die?

The funeral would be the next day, and while Karrie got ready for work, I sat on the recliner.

•

The day of the funeral was largely a blank. I have no words to express what was in my head, my heart, or anywhere inside me. It seemed that I had lived every day of my life until that day. Then on that day my life hit the pause button. And since that day I have come to live my life one day at a time.

---

3 Austin French, "Why God," on *Why God*. Fair Trade/Columbia, 2018.

Like the viewing, the funeral was packed out. And for anyone who grieves, many people paying their respects is very comforting.

Yet I didn't want to be there. Karrie practically forced me to go not just to the viewing but also to the funeral. I preferred to stay in my cave, a.k.a. recliner.

Through the whole order of service, my mind was a blank. I just went through the motions. We had the typical organ music, the eulogy, the message—but then came a rock-and-roll song, a favorite of Anissa's dad, Tony.

I took my last glimpse of Kirk's tousled tan hair, long eyelashes, and cute upturned nose—but under all that makeup.

Behind the hearse I rode in a limo from the funeral home to the graveside with Cody, Anissa, and Angie. Of all things to talk about, we talked about a trip to Nashville Cody and Anissa took when she was nine months pregnant and left the whole family scandalized. That and any other small talk served only as avoidance of what we were doing that day.

An endless line of cars followed the hearse and limo. Half the county seemed to have come.

And flowers. Flowers filled the funeral home. Flowers surrounded the graveside. If flowers could bring a person back to life, Kirk would have popped up like a jack-in-the-box.

•

In what would be the last time I was with Kirk, I met Anissa and Cody for dinner at a Mexican restaurant, a local favorite. Kirk ate chips and salsa with the rest of us. He liked tortilla chips with salsa, which seemed odd for such a young child because the salsa was spicy. But then he was our "Little Monster." He would let out a yelp to inform his mother that he hungered for another chip. He was just learning to speak a few words.

After dinner we headed out of the restaurant, and as soon as we passed through the doorway, off took Kirk down the sidewalk. Mom went in hot pursuit, and her commands to stop were to him like cheers to keep going. When Kirk paused to giggle, she finally apprehended the fleeing toddler.

I bent down and gave him a goodbye hug. I told him, "I love you."

He looked back into my eyes and said, "I wuve you."

This was my last memory of life with Kirk.

•

During the bereavement time I had off from work, I continued to sit immobilized on that recliner. Any inclination to do anything escaped me. Anyone who's had something most precious in life taken away can understand the inclination to do nothing because nothing matters anymore.

As the days passed, my emotional breakdowns got less frequent, and as I watched my wife go off to work, I gradually convinced myself that maybe it would be a good idea to return to daily a routine. And that poor old recliner wasn't going to last forever.

Yet even after I returned to work, whenever I got home, I went and sat immobilized on that recliner. Day after day. For months.

A month and a half into all that nothing, something happened. And it only made things worse.

My ex-wife brought her car in for service at the tire and auto repair shop where I worked. When I saw her, we walked out to the parking lot to catch up on how each of our children was doing. Then she asked, "Do you know anything about an investigation regarding Kirk's death?"

Huh? Investigation?

She waited for my response.

"No." I could only think, *Investigation? The babysitter said Kirk choked while eating eggs.*

We both stood there, and I abruptly said, "I've got to go."

I left the poor woman standing there and went straight to my office and called my friend who was a police detective.

CHAPTER 4

When Truth Is Worse than Lies

SMALL TOWNS THRIVE ON rumors, and talk is abundant when the story is good. The tales grow taller as they make their way from mouth to mouth, especially in a tragic event like this. The main one circulating was that the babysitter had been charged with a prior conviction of child neglect.

I was reluctant to get caught up in he-said-she-said. I needed confirmation from a reliable source. So when the ex-wife mentioned investigation, it got my attention.

I called a detective friend of mine in the local city police department and asked him if he could check into seeing if an investigation was taking place into the death of my grandson. I knew that if there was an investigation, it would be handled by the county sheriff's department. He said he would check for me. Less than an hour later he called back.

"Yes, Dave, there is an investigation going on into Kirk's death."

Oh my.

"A friend of mine is handling the case. He's a good detective."

My heart sank once again. I was almost in shock.

Part of me didn't want to believe it was anything but an accident. The idea that Kirk was killed cut too deeply into my heart to even want to think about.

Then a rumor circulated of allegations that the babysitter had abused her own children when they were young. On one hand, this was confirming as to where the whole situation was pointing. On the other hand, I wished none of it were true.

The alleged abuse of her own kids was never officially recorded. But the prior conviction was.

One evening a text message came from Anissa to my wife concerning information about the babysitter. The woman had indeed been previously charged with a prior criminal offense.

We asked Anissa to provide us with the name of the babysitter so we could further investigate. Karrie and I entered her name into the search engine, and sure enough, after looking through a few websites, it appeared.

Kirk's babysitter had been charged with felony battery and child neglect. But in a plea bargain the charges were reduced to misdemeanor child neglect. She only served one year of probation. How could such a deal be possible?

This person also turned out to be the mother of the guy at the viewing who asked us to go visit his mother. It was *her*. She had been Kirk's babysitter. And the guy at the viewing would have been one of her three children she allegedly abused.

Anissa didn't think it would be appropriate for us to visit her. Nor did we.

•

Melba, Angie's mother-in-law and Anissa's grandmother, told us that the babysitter had been her friend. Melba had been an Avon representative, and in her sales work had gotten to know the babysitter over a long time. So she had recommended her to Anissa. But neither of them knew about the babysitter's past. And no one else bringing kids to the babysitter's home daycare knew about her past either.

Only after talking to Angie, Anissa, and the rest of the family did I find out that prior to the funeral, the police had conducted interviews with Anissa, Cody, Anissa's parents, and Anissa's sister, Anndrea. They had been told to not say anything, and they didn't.

My wife and I were never interviewed. I'm guessing that's because we were in Florida at the time and because Kirk never lived with us.

Anissa said that when the nurses saw Kirk come in, they could tell right away he had not choked to death.

When she arrived, Anissa wasn't allowed to pick him up and got yelled at for touching his hair. But a compassionate nurse, who said she wasn't supposed to, allowed Anissa to spend a couple of minutes with Kirk. Then someone pulled Anissa away.

Why wouldn't the police allow Anissa to hold Kirk's body—her own son! It seemed harsh to the point of misconduct.

But now it made sense.

The mysteries and confusing pieces of the story started falling into place.

And we all began to wonder what *really* happened that terrible Wednesday morning.

And at the viewing, what was all that thick coroner's makeup on Kirk's face covering up? And why did the funeral home employees monitor the casket and ask us to not touch Kirk's face because it would distort the makeup?

•

Answers again. I needed answers. Losing a loved one already feels impossible. We can come to accept death as an accident. And maybe even accept it as God's will. But to discover that the death of our beloved was at the hands of another person—this plunges an already life-altering tragedy to a far deeper level. The answers to that linger out of reach.

I spoke with the case detective, and he assured me that he would keep me informed. But he also said he couldn't talk about the investigation because it was ongoing. So I just had to wait.

It seemed as if time stood still during the investigation. Angie and I had similar thinking on this whole thing, and we talked and wondered about things together: When would the case be turned over to the prosecutor's office? When would an arrest be made? What charges would be brought against the babysitter?

Our questions intensified after Angie and Anissa talked with the mother of the child whom the babysitter had been convicted of neglecting.

The babysitter had claimed that during a naptime, the little boy's blanket had gotten wrapped around his neck, where it blocked both blood and oxygen to his brain.

But it appeared to the mother that the reddish marks on the neck were not those of a blanket but looked more like markings of hands or fingers. It seemed that the mother didn't hire a lawyer or pursue the allegations beyond her initially reporting it.

The mother couldn't prove what happened. No one could. So the babysitter successfully plea-bargained from a felony battery charge down to misdemeanor neglect.

Only after that did the baby start having seizures. For the rest of his life, he would have to take medication to counter the seizures that apparently began because of this babysitter's gross neglect, or worse.

And as before, we had more questions than answers.

•

Day after day, night after night, I spent transfixed on the same picture of Kirk. I re-experienced my ride to the airport in Florida, plane trip to Chicago, ride home from O'Hare, and went back to staring at Kirk's picture. I kept imagining he would climb out of that screen and sit on my lap just one more time.

As the grieving process eased and normal daily routines retook their place, I noticed in that photo what I had always seen but not seen. A bruise on his left cheek. I know I had to have noticed it before, but now it took on a new significance.

I took a new look at other photos of him. He's in a green striped shirt, riding a merry-go-round, his mother's hand around his waist. And there it is: a different bruise, this one on his right cheek.

I pull up the always-endearing mealtime photo. He's sitting in a highchair, wearing a white shirt, with his face and hands covered in fruit juice and pieces of fruit. But on his messy little face is a yet another bruise, this one near his left eye.

It seems illogical that no one ever previously pieced things together. But as Angie and Anissa shared more pictures with us, the endless bruises became alarmingly evident. In nearly every photo he had a bruise somewhere on his body.

Why had we never before seen what we saw now?

Yes, we had actually noticed them before—we weren't blind.

But we *were* blind to why.

Whenever Anissa or Angie or anyone else noticed a bruise and asked about it, the babysitter always had an explanation: He fell off a couch. Another child hit him with a car. He ran into the wall. He was rambunctious.

Every bruise came with a new explanation. And for an energetic toddler nicknamed "Little Monster" or "Little Monkey," the explanations seemed reasonable.

Now they echoed like screams, every word a lie.

And after hearing what the mother of the previously injured boy alleged, we could easily imagine that the babysitter may have been covering her actions with excuses in Kirk's case as well.

We could only imaging the violence he—and the other kids—had endured day after day after day.

CHAPTER 5

Hoping for Justice

THE DETECTIVE WOULDN'T TALK about the investigation because it was ongoing. We understood, but we were still frustrated at how much time it was taking. And I was frustrated at the way I was learning everything second hand.

Finally we met with the prosecuting attorney herself. She gave us as much of an update as she could. And she assured us that the process was moving along. They needed a very thorough investigation to assure a conviction. "Making sure that all the *t*'s are crossed and the *i*'s are dotted," is the way she explained it. Once the investigation was complete, it would be turned over to her. During the meeting I remember thinking, as we questioned her, that she was very confident and determined. Things like this bring a kind of comfort through the hope of justice to grieving families.

Whenever something in life seems wrong, human instinct is to want to make it right. That may mean to fix it, or it may mean to seek vengeance. When another person hurts us, our nature is to want to hurt them back. Personally, I see no comfort in that philosophy.

I do, on the other hand, believe that our judicial system should punish an individual who has broken the law, whether that person has harmed another person or not. So in our case, what would be achieved by the prosecution's intent to take away the babysitter's freedom? Obviously, she would not be able to repeat her offence against another child. And she wouldn't get away with hurting other inmates. So my grieving was helped by the fact that while she would be incarcerated, she could not harm another child.

I am also grateful that other people had suspicions. If they hadn't, there would have been no investigation or prosecution, and Kirk's life would have been taken by an individual who effortlessly got away by the acceptance of her story. Even before any verdict, the fact that others noticed and went to great lengths to investigate also gives me comfort.

Seeing T-shirts that read "Justice for K" also brought comfort by showing that our family was not alone. Support of the community can be a tremendous lift to anyone in grief. Most people who grieve do not receive broad communal support, and receiving it is a gift for which I am grateful.

For anyone going through grief of whatever kind, it is important to acknowledge and appreciate circumstances and people that in different ways bring comfort or encouragement. Without doing so, we easily get buried in self-oriented sorrow. And when we do so, we are lifted up and strengthened to go forward.

·

The prosecuting attorney grew to be a trusted authority for us, and even friend. So we started calling her by her first name, Vicki.

She finally informed us that the investigation's *t*'s all got crossed and the *i*'s all got dotted. We had a completed investigation.

What struck me most was that Kirk's death was ruled a homicide. *Homicide.* My first thought went to *murder.* Yet homicide, I learned, was an umbrella term for any killing of a person by another person. Some homicides, like killing of an armed suspect by a police officer or killing in self-defense, are considered lawful. Murder and manslaughter are unlawful.

The actual charge was "battery resulting in the death of a child under the age of fourteen." A conviction would carry a maximum of up to thirty years in prison. The minimum was ten years. Thirty years was a long time, but ten years—probably serving seven of them—seemed like a slap on the wrist compared to life without Kirk.

As much confidence as I had been feeling up till now suddenly slipped into serious doubt. I had expected a more serious charge, like second-degree murder or at least manslaughter, even involuntary manslaughter.

We questioned her about this. It was a felony charge, but it seemed too light.

She explained that the burden of proof was much greater for a charge like murder or manslaughter. Thus it would have been less likely to succeed. Though the prosecution had a good case, they didn't want to take any chances of losing, which would have handed the babysitter an acquittal. The prospect of seeing the babysitter walk free from more severe charges was a worst-case scenario that none of us wanted.

She was confident that the battery charge would gain a conviction.

One other factor would possibly play a part. In a court trial the prosecution is not allowed to bring up a defendant's prior convictions during court proceedings—namely the babysitter's plea-bargained misdemeanor child neglect. The only way it can be addressed is if the defense or the accused admits it or falsely claims not to have had a prior conviction or to have done things they in fact did. But a prior conviction can, and always is, considered in sentencing.

Vicki may have been thinking that because the babysitter had that prior conviction of abuse, if she secured a conviction in this case, the babysitter would probably receive the maximum sentence of thirty years.

Thirty years is a long, long, time, and at the babysitter's age, if she served the full thirty years, it would equate to the same thing as a life sentence.

Our confidence in Vicki was restored.

Buoyed by this development, I called the news station to tell them an arrest would be made at the babysitter's home. After a one-day delay, the news media was all over the arrest and splashed the news across northern Indiana.

•

The first pretrial hearing was scheduled and conducted. Now we were getting somewhere.

The charges were brought against the defendant: Battery resulting in the death of a child under the age of fourteen. She pleaded not guilty.

Then the judge set a trial date. Cases got put on the docket in the order that they went to prosecution, and the prosecutor said there were at least six cases ahead of Kirk's. But court congestion would quickly make this date meaningless. Most likely, the rescheduled trial date would confront still more delays.

The bond was set at only $100,000. The babysitter posted bail and didn't spend any time incarcerated.

Vicki explained that an incarcerated person had the right to a speedy trial within seventy days. So as other people were arrested and did not post bail, their cases would receive priority and bump our trial date back even further. On the other hand, if a plea bargain were agreed upon, a case wouldn't go to trial. So a trial could be moved up the list because of plea bargains or move down the list because of others' rights to a speedy trial.

For those who wait, it is an emotional roller coaster.

•

So there she was, day after day, taking care of her house, living her life, even going to the fair. Perhaps we should have been more charitable about a person's innocence before being proven guilty, but our sense of injustice was greater, and we felt sick about it.

While we felt comforted by the hope of justice, the process was taking excruciatingly long. Whatever they were doing or not doing became maddening. Without blaming law enforcement or the judicial system, sometimes things do take a long time.

Whatever the reasons for investigation or court delays, families who've lost loved ones to criminal activity know all too well this pain of waiting. The emotions can feel like hanging high in the air by a nasty hook, day and night, never knowing whether or when you'll be set down gently in soft grass or dropped mercilessly into a pit of spears.

We waited for months.

And the waiting would stretch for *two years*.

Thankfully we had Angie. And while we waited, she took charge of pursuing another kind of justice.

CHAPTER 6

Kirk's Law—a Blessing from Tragedy

ANGIE AND I HAD the same thought. There had to be legislation to prevent Kirk's tragedy from happening again.

In the State of Indiana, convicted sexual offenders' names, photos, and addresses were listed on a public online registry. Anyone concerned or wishing to inquire could do so at their fingertips. But nothing like this existed regarding those convicted of crimes against children.

Angie took action and contacted our local state representative for a meeting. He graciously met with her and discussed ideas about legislation to prevent child abuse crimes in the future.

They also discussed the idea of state licenses for childcare providers. Indiana does not require a state license to perform childcare in one's personal residence. Why? Because a law requiring state licensing for every childcare provider would drastically reduce the amount of providers available, which would cause more problems.

A person was only limited to how many children they could babysit at their home. Babysitters who had a state license were preferred, but unlicensed providers tended to be less costly.

The choice for Kirk's childcare was that the babysitter was a friend of the family. And because the babysitter was a trusted family friend, state licensing wasn't a concern. But we had no way of checking to be sure. If we had, Kirk would never have gone to that babysitter.

•

A few weeks later, with Angie taking the lead, we connected with our local state senator, Carlin Yoder. I was unable to attend this meeting, and Yoder later indicated that he was initially skeptical about whether he could help develop something positive in response to Kirk's death. But after hearing the passion and pain that the family was feeling, he knew he had to act in some way to ensure that, from a state perspective, they did everything they could to prevent this from happening again. Meeting them even in their home, he was amazed by the resolve the family showed. He said, "They were adamant that something needed to happen and were not going to sit by idly and hope that we would act. This determination was all I needed to do everything I could to develop what turned into Kirk's Law."

Of the process, Yoder said, "I struggled for a while to come up with the right way to develop the idea of a child abuse registry. We debated who should be in charge of it and who should pay for the cost to develop it and maintain it. I had incredible support from fellow legislators, and many wanted to get on board as a co-author. We had no opposition from any legislators and only token pushback from individuals who felt it could be an invasion of privacy to have names placed on a public list."

Yoder soon drafted what became Bill 357, and it headed for the Senate Judiciary Committee at the State House in Indianapolis. We were as grateful as we were amazed at how this was happening. And we wanted to spare other families from the same heartache.

If passed, the bill would work much like a sex offender registry as a public, electronic database. It would be a child abuse registry established under state court administration. And it would detail the convicted offender's name, age, last known city of residence, a photograph if available, a description of the crime of child abuse conviction, and any other identifying information as determined by the court division involved. Anyone convicted of a felony against a child, whether child neglect, battery, sexual abuse, physical abuse, or the like, would be listed on this public online registry.

The essence of the bill's text started by describing the crimes addressed under existing criminal codes, including neglect of a dependent child, child selling, sex offense, battery against a child causing bodily injury, or battery against a child causing serious bodily injury or death.

The bill went on to say that the registry shall be published on the division's internet website, and that it must be searchable and available to the public. Also, the registry is to be updated every thirty days.

The closing statement of the bill read: "Based on information submitted to law enforcement, a person whose name appears in this registry has been convicted of a crime of child abuse. However, information on the registry may not be complete."

There it was—pain and loss making its way to redemption and, hopefully, reality.

Angie bravely stood in front of the committee and testified by telling our story of Kirk. Others testified also. But the estimated cost to create and maintain a registry could be $300,000 a year. Senate Judiciary Chair Brent Steele promised to find a way to pay for it. "I don't care about the fiscal impact," said Senator Greg Taylor, "When it comes to the safety of children, I don't care if we have to spend a million dollars." When the vote was taken, the committee members passed it 100 percent.

The bill moved on to the senate floor for deliberation and a vote. And once again, it passed 100 percent with bipartisan approval, not one single vote opposing.

•

Now the bill went to the Committee on Courts and Criminal Code. Once again Angie testified in front of the committee. The committee voted 100 percent in favor.

The bill moved on to the house of representatives floor for deliberation and a vote. Again, a bipartisan 100 percent voted in favor.

Finally the bill reached the governor's desk. And the governor? Mike Pence, then governor of Indiana, indicated his intention to sign the bill. We would now have a new state law, and it would be named "Kirk's Law."

All this happened while we waited and waited for a trial.

We were amazed at the contrasts of how governmental wheels could turn so differently.

But we were more amazed that we—especially Angie and little Kirk who was allowed to be nothing more than a victim—could make a difference like this for so many others.

•

We all have a view of politicians, and unfortunately, most are not very positive. I had heard good things about our governor. And months prior to the signing, we actually met him when leaving the State House. We were on our way out of the committee meeting as he came our way. I recognized him and walked up to him to shake his hand. He was very cordial.

I would meet Governor Pence again at the ceremonial signing of Kirk's Law. The day of the signing, I thought the event would probably be a perfunctory fifteen-minute ceremony. But it turned out to be a once-in-a-lifetime experience.

After being interviewed by the *Crime Watch Daily* show, I went to find a seat in the Town Hall of Middlebury, Indiana, where the bill would be signed. The room was filled with supporters and local news reporters. But before I could locate a seat, all of the family members were called into a small break room.

The governor arrived, and straight to the break room he went. His assistant said, "No reporters," and closed the door. We introduced ourselves, and the governor hugged all the women and shook hands with all us guys. Then he said a prayer, yes the governor said a *prayer*. And he told his assistant, "Put on a pot of coffee." Next he said, "Tell me about Kirk." For the next fifteen minutes we shared stories of Kirk. The governor was so sincere and so genuinely caring about us. This was an important and busy man who took part of his precious time to spend with us. As I said, it was a once in a lifetime experience.

After the signing, Governor Pence stayed and visited with us *again*. And he was very patient as we took pictures with him. This man who would become Vice President Mike Pence was, and would always be, a truly unique and genuinely wonderful person.

What I thought would be a show up, sign, take pictures, and duck out quickly, was instead profoundly surprising.

The bill, now Kirk's Law, would go into effect just after the babysitter was scheduled to stand trial.

Then the trial began.

CHAPTER 7

Closure Eludes Us

DURING MEETINGS WITH VICKI before the trial, we discussed the question of a plea bargain. She explained that the longer that it took for a defendant to agree to a plea bargain, the less likely it would be agreed upon. If the defendant wanted to plea bargain, the earlier he entered a plea, the better an agreement he would get. We all had mixed feelings about it the idea. We would not have to go through the pain and heartache of reliving the events through a trial. But a plea-bargained sentence would certainly be lighter. Yet if we went to trial, there was always the possibility of a not-guilty decision.

I can only speculate as to why the babysitter, who had previously done a plea bargain, wanted a trial as opposed to a plea bargain this time. Do people who think they're innocent of a charge filed against them consider a plea bargain to be a viable option? Or if they deep down know they're guilty, do they consider themselves able to outwit investigations and escape the law? Or do they prefer to gamble their lives? Vicki said of the babysitter in one of our meetings,

"She is in denial." The woman must have been deep in denial if she actually thought a jury would acquit her.

•

The court delays were finally over, and we had a firm trial date. Finally we'd find closure. All along we all had thoughts about what happened that tragic Wednesday, and they circulated quietly and safely contained in the backs of our minds. As much as we waited on justice, it could only come after those events and thoughts were released to do battle in the courtroom. The thought of it horrified me.

We now sat in a packed little courtroom. It was an important case in the county and had gotten a lot of attention, so the place was filled to overflowing.

Then the jury walked in. As they filed into their seats, it didn't appear to me to be a favorable jury. More men than women, and only two younger women. I was hoping for more younger women to identify with Kirk's mother. We'd see.

The prosecution and the defense made their opening statements. Then the first witness was called to the stand—Angie.

As Angie was sworn in, I thought of how courageous she had been on the podium during the process of passing Kirk's Law. My thoughts turned to compassion as Vicki stood and asked Angie to relive Kirk's final two days. I could only imagine what would be going through my mind if I were in her place, perched in front of a crowded room filled with family, friends, strangers, reporters, highly educated professionals, a jury, and supporting members and family of the babysitter. "Frightening" could only begin to explain my emotions as I processed Angie's every word.

To Angie's right stood a big projector screen. I don't recall how loud my gasp was as Angie was asked to identity that little orange shirt Kirk was wearing that morning as it appeared on that screen, a screen that seemed a thousand times bigger than it actually was. I do recall my younger sister Diane grasping my leg in an attempt to either console or silence me, probably both. I squeezed my eyes shut, wanting nothing more than to make that image disappear. I could only hang my head and wait for the next question in hopes that the screen would return to its original state of blank white when I unclenched my eyes.

Vicki went through the normal events of Kirk's last day, including all the typical taking-care-of-kid things they did the previous night and the regular morning routine of getting him up, putting on his clothes, and bringing him to the babysitter's. Everything was normal—nothing indicated anything was wrong with Kirk when we went to the babysitter's.

Then the defense took up questioning and went through a vague review with Angie of everything Vicki had addressed. The attorney was probably looking for discrepancies.

Then we went to a recess.

During the recess Vicki told us she would try to get us moved to the larger courtroom upstairs for the next day's continuation of the trial.

Then we squeezed back into the courtroom, even having to fight over seats, and sat down.

Vicki stood. Instead of continuing the case, she requested that the Coleman and Garza families meet outside the courtroom.

We knew Vicki had things under control, so we were curious about what was going on. As we shuffled out, I thought maybe the babysitter had changed her mind and wanted to plea bargain. In that case we wouldn't have to go through the trial.

We followed Vicki out to the lobby and gathered closely as we silently looking at each other. Everyone else had a look of positive anticipation as well.

I waited for good news.

Vicki stood before us and abruptly said, "The case has been declared a mistrial."

WHAT?

In an instant it felt as if a silent stun bomb had been dropped on us all. Every face in shock, no one said a word.

Vicki calmly and confidently continued. "During the recess, a juror mentioned the babysitter's prior conviction to the other jurors." The news stations would later call this "tainting the jury," a form of jury misconduct that caused the declaration of a mistrial.

Really? A juror makes one comment, and it throws the whole trial out the window?

We all knew the prior conviction was not admissible during the trial. And we were all upset about this because it was a major piece of background information.

The only way it would be admissible was if the babysitter were on the witness stand and stated that she hadn't done anything like this before.

Vicki said that there was no way that her attorney would allow her to admit anything like that.

So after waiting two years for a court date, we had another delay. A new trial had to be scheduled. How much more disappointment do families have to endure?

"I will let you know when it gets rescheduled. For now, leave immediately and go straight to your vehicles. Do not talk to any reporters until after the story is on the news. Just go home."

That allowed us to leave before it was publicly announced in the courtroom and swarms of people and reporters would pour out.

I had a truckload of questions. Yet even without answers, I trusted her.

Because of the passing of Kirk's Law, she was always concerned about the attention the case itself was getting from the news outlets, particularly the nationally syndicated *Crime Watch Daily* show.

The next day's *Goshen News* reported Vicki's reaction to the mistrial: "Definitely not happy. Quite frankly, devastated. Everybody from both sides are waiting to get this case resolved, and having something like this happen just delays further."

I assumed that the more attention the case got, the more likely a change of venue might be entered by the defense. Yet during our meetings, Vicki was confident that no change of venue would be granted. As I reflect back, I think it was a big concern to her, but she didn't want us to be worried.

•

So, the long agonizing wait for a trial was again extended. Other family members said, "She needs to pay for her actions. Lock her up and throw away the key." I understood their pain. I felt their pain. There was indeed satisfaction in the thought of her locked up. But would it bring back our beloved Kirk? No. We all knew that. Was it a proper punishment for what she was accused of doing? Yes. If she were found guilty by a jury of her peers, her freedom would be taken. The whole process was compelling evidence that we are an imperfect society of laws, working as best as we can, and that our morals are always on trial—whether we sit in the witness stand or sit in the gallery.

Facts rule over everything said in a courtroom. The prosecution and defense find and expose facts. The judge rules over the presentation of these facts. And facts can be presented, emphasized, deemphasized, and manipulated one way or the other.

Then enter the twelve-person jury—human beings just like you and me. How are they to make a decision about another person's future? They aren't judges. They aren't prosecutors. And they aren't lawyers. They're normal people. This was where I struggled with the thought that this person, the babysitter, could potentially walk out of the courtroom a free woman. I tried to prepare myself for that possibility. It only took one of those twelve jurors—just one—to find reasonable doubt about the events that took place on that October day. Not the judge nor the prosecutor nor the defense lawyer could make the decision. I was solely relying on the outcome of the trial, itself dependent on these free-willed human beings, to receive redemption for life without Kirk.

But can a court trial ever be a truly adequate means of redemption? The more I thought about it, the more I recognized that courts were good for *retribution*. And one always hopes they will be good for achieving justice. But *redemption*? That's another matter—one I would find in my own life.

CHAPTER 8

Finding Faith

I SEARCHED AND SEARCHED for an answer—for redemption—through my jumbled, mind-bending thoughts of how a nineteen-month-old child's life could be snuffed out like that.

Somewhere in the midst of it all, I started considering *myself*. And it started occurring to me that *I* needed redemption. So I gradually started looking to something bigger than myself, bigger than the situation, and bigger than the pain.

•

The prequel to this occurred when my children were young, and their mother wanted us all to attend church. The boys had attended preschool at a local Lutheran church, so we started going to Sunday services there. She was still a member in her hometown, so it was just a transfer of membership for her. I met with the pastor to initiate my membership. In my adulthood, Sunday sermons always aroused my curiosity. But membership was different. I told the Pastor that I did not see myself worthy enough to become part of the congregation. I had not lived my life as a Christian, and I knew I would fail if I tried. I was a good provider for my family, and I was mature enough to realize that I now could live out my life obeying the Ten Commandments, but my vision of a Christian *lifestyle* was out of reach for me.

As it turned out our attending Sunday services was short lived, not due to my reluctance to join but by an event that took place in the aisle of the sanctuary. During each service the children were called to the front for a short story. One Sunday Chad rose and started toward the front, but Cody, being as competitive as his father, would not allow his older brother to beat him, so he tackled him to the carpet right there in the aisle. A little wrestling match ensued as I sunk down in my seat, head buried in my hands. Figuring this kind of thing would happen again, we were too embarrassed to go back.

Now, years later, I realize the importance of forgiveness and working things out over any vain attempt to be perfect. Romans 3:23 says, "All have sinned and fall short of the glory of God." All of us. I learned, needed, to receive God's forgiveness—and work things out in my own life.

•

Two influencers along my life's timeline nudged me back onto the path toward God.

A friend that I had known for twenty-five years stopped into my place of work. Larry had always been a little cocky, but this time he was different. He spoke to me about Jesus and how he had received Jesus as his personal Savior. Hmmm . . . But whatever I may have thought, he was so different from before! He apologized if he had ever said anything to offend me in the past. Larry has truly been a godsend to me. Even now he sends me a Bible verse every day. He takes no credit for all he has done for me. The most important thing Larry has shown me is how, through his faith, he was transformed from being prideful and self righteousness—which we're all guilty of—to being humble with a servant's attitude toward others, and most importantly, to serving Jesus Christ. Whenever I thank him, he says, "It's God working through me." God Bless Larry.

Will is another blessing whom God sent to me. Will came into my life as a customer. He was having vibration issues with his vehicle. We rebalanced his tires, and I told him to drive and make sure the vibration was gone. He was greatly appreciative of the service. I don't recall exactly when he spoke to me about Jesus, but he planted a seed. What is it about meeting a stranger that makes you feel as if you've known them your entire life? I believe God amazingly arranges these meetings for us. I initially was drawn to Will's beaming personality. And after a few conversations, it was as if I could see his heart. He was a man of God.

I was learning to appreciate and wanting to emulate both his and Larry's passion for Christ. I could clearly sense that I was moving closer to God. One of these men re-entered my life a changed person and one entered a stranger. Both inspired me on my journey of faith.

I had never thought I was good enough to be a Christian. Then as I thought through my life, I increasingly realized that nobody is. Jesus died for us *because* we're not perfect.

•

The person who brought me along to encounter and receive the living Christ was my oldest brother, Kim. It happened during the interlude between the mistrial and the trial to come. Kim was also facing adversity in his life, as we all do, and apparently feeling nudged himself, he started attending church. One day his pastor came to the tire shop, and I liked him. So I decided I would also like to try the church. The pastor was from California and was a cool-type dude, not your typical image of a pastor. His messages were down to earth and based on Scripture. I grew to find this very important to me.

I've heard people say they took a leap of faith. I didn't leap; I walked. Or more accurately, I crawled.

As I crawled and picked up the pieces of my shattered life, I realized it was beneficial to let God in on my problems. Inch by inch I moved toward putting my life under God's authority. To put it another way, I slowly began giving ultimate control of my life over to God until you could say I finally made a life commitment to Jesus. As I did that, I began growing in this newfound faith. I also learned to appreciate God's grace, his unmerited love for us all. And when adversity arose, this is where I asked God to take control, "Jesus, Take the Wheel," as the Carrie Underwood song goes.

And when I was the cause of problems, I pleaded his mercy.

Due to some family complications, my brother needed to find a different church. He told me this new church had an intriguing and thought-provoking pastor and that I had to check this guy out. So I followed my brother there as well. This pastor was also very down to earth, based his messages on Scripture, and addressed current events we face today. After a service I told him that he touched me deep down in my soul and that I felt he had "God's gift of cleansing souls"—at least mine! I started seeing a difference in my brother as well.

My crawl developing into a walk and then a pace my mind could barely keep up with. And I thank these two pastors for their part in my life transformation.

I felt as if Jesus were asleep in me for all these years—and what awoke in me was the grace of God, who knew me and loved me even before I responded. At times my spiritual awareness awakened but never came alive in an embracing, living relationship with this Creator God who manifested himself in the figure of Jesus Christ and who is actually present within me through his Holy Spirit. But now it did. Blows my mind whenever I think about it.

•

In addition to faith, my story also has a villain. But I began to ask this: Who is the *true* villain of my story?

I can honestly say that my own temper has, many times, gotten the best of me. I just give thanks that it hasn't resulted in the loss of anyone's life. If I were to put myself in the babysitter's place, how would I handle it? As empathetic as I like to think of myself, I found that identifying with her position was extremely difficult to even consider. As Vicki said, "She is in denial." Is it possible for a person's subconscious to block out an event that completely? Where is the moving line between denial and narcissistic dishonesty? I will never know the answer to that.

What if your actions were responsible for a young person's death—such as a car accident? As human beings, some of us tend to sink into guilt, and some of us tend to justify ourselves. At a training class for work, the instructor made this comment: "If we cannot justify our position in life, we will end it." So do we have a built-in self-justifying instinct right beside a self-condemning instinct? Subconsciously, do we both protect ourselves and attack ourselves? And does one take over at limits of the other?

Did the babysitter consider herself a villain protecting herself? It seemed to me, based on events, that she was in denial she would do such a thing, and her outward action was self-preservation. If I were in her situation, I think I would have thrown myself at the mercy of the judge, pleaded guilty, and received my sentence. I would not even have plea-bargained because I would have admitted full guilt and received my due punishment. But how do I really know? A self-preservation instinct might have risen up in me too.

I've always thought of my self as a good person, yet I found myself being drawn, or tempted, to go down paths of what one could call the dark side. I found myself wanting to do all kinds of vengeful things to the babysitter and hire a hit man to put her to death without incriminating myself. The simple fact that I even thought these things deeply troubled me. What kind of person was I? I realized that if I allowed myself to be continually tempted and drawn down that dark path, I might become no different from the babysitter. I could even become worse.

If we pause to think about what goes on in the world or in bad situations we confront, even in the depths of our own hearts, bad character traits can develop from bad decisions that people, including ourselves, may make early in life. But that cannot be all. Some things go beyond anyone's natural character into a darkness, a negative force, independent of humans, that is prevalent everywhere and all through history.

The days came back to me when Mom and Dad dropped us off for free babysitting at the Baptist Sunday school. Thinking back on the church's teaching gave me the impression that I had better believe in God if I didn't want to burn in hell. And now it started coming clear to me that there really was an identifiable force, even a personal force—which along with the Bible's teaching, is commonly known as the devil, along with all his demonic spirits. Was it my childhood image of a bad guy in a red suit with a pitchfork who tempted me to be bad? No, I started to see that the personification of evil and darkness in the world and in my own life was darker and more wicked than I was capable of imagining.

I have to conclude, then, that the true villain of this story is not the babysitter at all. Behind her, as behind much of the darkness in the world and in our own hearts, is the deception of what is known as the devil.

Grasping all this helped me realize that many people allow themselves to go down a dark path, even if they don't intend it. Grasping this also awakened me to clearly recognize that I needed to consciously stay off that path and go the other way toward my newfound faith in God.

So the devastating things the family and I went through pressed me into this most precious gift of recognizing God in my life. It was like a trough of manure sprouting a beautiful, fragrant flower. I'm grateful that my faith wasn't only that of the happy flower but also included the other side of faith that recognizes the reality, even personification, of spiritual darkness and evil in the present world and beyond.

This new reality in my life then carried me through the trial to come.

CHAPTER 9

Closure Arrives

ON THIS SECOND TIME around, the trial was moved to a much larger courtroom. Even then it was packed throughout the entire three-day duration. I watched the jury a lot. One lady sat there looking detached the whole trial. She seemed to have made up her mind already—one way or the other. She made me nervous.

The babysitter's younger son—the tall, dark-haired man who spoke so supportively of her at Kirk's viewing—turned silent after charges were filed. And I didn't even see him at either the first trial or this one. That seemed telling.

The defense attorney was dressed to kill in a dark suit and tie. Vicky, in her skirt and flowered blouse, looked too casual by comparison. But as the trial began, I realized that what each of them had inside was the opposite of how they dressed. Homework and preparation trump appearance.

Court documents stated that the babysitter called 911 and told the dispatcher that the boy was choking. Then he later died.

And whenever a child dies, there's a mandatory autopsy.

Enter the pathologist. That person examined Kirk during the awful time when no one was allowed to touch him. As this trial did not get derailed by any mishaps, we finally got to hear the report.

The pathologist found no evidence that Kirk died from choking. Rather, he concluded that Kirk died from "blunt force trauma" and that he had "significant head injuries" to his "brain, optic nerves, and both retinas." He was hit hard, really hard. On top of that, the report noted that Kirk had sustained a previous injury on the right side of his head.

The defense attorney did not put up much of a case, nor did he cross-examine very hard. He did little more than try to discredit the points of the prosecution. Vicki was very aggressive on her main points that Kirk was as normal as could be when they dropped him off in the morning, and that the babysitter was the only one who could possibly have caused Kirk's death. She also emphasized how no one in Kirk's family had any indication or record of being abusive. On other less-important points, she seemed passive, like someone picking and choosing her battles.

Without many objections, the proceedings went smoothly from one point to another.

On the last day Vicki graduated herself to a killer dark blazer to drive home her case.

•

The babysitter had to have known it was just a matter of time that the truth would come out.

Because autopsies don't lie.

54

She had EMT training. Her husband was a member of the local fire department, and he had to have had EMT training as well. Although it would never come out at the trial, the first phone call made, according to the babysitter's phone records, was not to 911, but to her husband. He was the first one on the scene, and this was confirmed by his testimony at the trial. Surely he knew what took place that dreadful morning. A trained EMT had to have known that the choking claim would not pass investigation. And as I heard the husband's testimony, it had to be unfavorable toward his wife's defense. He testified that when he arrived, he found no sign of anything blocking the airway. I'll never know, but I can't help but speculate that if after reviewing the case files, her attorney recommended that she attempt a plea bargain. If he did, it must have fallen on deaf ears.

Thoughts swirled around my head of how the babysitter had been charged with felony battery of a child and had plea-bargained down to a misdemeanor. And how the child would spend the rest of his life on medication to counter the seizures because of it. And how the mother thought the marks on her boy's neck looked more like those of fingers, not a blanket. All that information in this trial would have nailed the babysitter's coffin shut in short order. But it was off limits as admissible evidence unless the babysitter took the stand and indicated she had never committed any kind of abuse to a child. Only then could Vicki have addressed it. The defense attorney would have been a fool to let that happen.

So we'd see an outcome based only on Kirk's fate.

As it was, the jury deliberated for an hour and a half. Not long at all by normal standards. But with anxiety running high, it still felt like forever. We went to dinner and tried to feel normal, but everything on the menu was nothing but a variation of anxiety. While still at the restaurant, we got the call that the jury had reached a verdict.

I took it as a good sign that the quicker they made a decision, the more likely it would be the decision I was hoping for.

We walked back to the courtroom and sat down.

Within minutes the jury entered and took their seats. And with no further procedures or even comments, Judge Cataldo asked, "Ladies and gentlemen of the jury, have you reached a verdict?"

The foreman of jury stood. "Yes, your honor." He handed an envelope to the bailiff, who passed it to the judge.

She read it and pronounced, "The jury finds the defendant guilty as charged."

Our whole family gasped, and I think we all started crying tears of joy.

Our torturous two-year journey since losing Kirk was finally over. Now we could start to move forward again. And we would carry Kirk in our hearts with a sense of justice having been done twice over—Kirk's Law and this conviction.

"Relieved. Relieved," Angie told the media. "Justice was finally served."

We had to wait another month for sentencing. Yet to me, just knowing the lady was found guilty was enough for now.

•

The sentencing happened on schedule a month later—amazing that we got no delays.

All we knew going in was that the sentence would be between ten and thirty years. I didn't expect her to get the maximum but only hoped she'd get twenty or twenty-five.

Both sides crammed into opposite sides of a room at the county jail, and the babysitter sat behind glass in an adjacent room.

A neighbor, who was never called as a witness in the trial, stood to give his opinion that the babysitter was a good person, a good neighbor, and that he didn't think she would hurt a child. On the babysitter's behalf, someone read a few letters people had sent in support of her.

After that Angie spoke about our family's loss. Then I read a statement to Judge Cataldo that expressed the family's grief, in part conveyed through these excerpts:

As winter weather is upon us, it deeply saddens us that we have been denied the opportunities to build snowmen, make snow angels and sled down snow-covered hills with our beloved Kirk. What we thought would be the first of many Christmases with Kirk, was heart-breakingly his last. . . . Sadly the times we wept will now outweigh those memories that could have been, and those precious memories we do have will forever stay afloat on those tears. . . . Yet we feel holding a grudge can be detrimental to the healing process, so we look to Matthew 6:14, "For if you forgive other people when they Sin against you, your Heavenly Father will also forgive you."

Though we knew the importance of personal forgiveness, particularly the releasing of anger or hatred, the objective of justice was a different matter. Thus in closing I read,

We have prayerfully and tearfully written, to petition you to rule that she receives the maximum sentence that the state allows.

Then came the sentencing. The judge briefly noted in her consideration that the babysitter had a prior conviction of child neglect. After all this time I had forgotten that the prior conviction was admissible in sentencing. But indeed it was. Judge Cataldo concluded that in light of this, she would sentence the babysitter to the maximum sentence of thirty years.

And there it was: a final verdict and judgment.

On one hand, I felt happy. On the other hand, thirty years would be a very long time for this wife, mother, and grandmother to be separated from her family. Yet life without Kirk would last a lifetime.

Her new address would be at the women's state penitentiary.

•

Then came another delay. The babysitter appealed. The appeal asked for her conviction to be overturned or for a reduction in her sentencing or that she be given a new trial or new sentencing.

Her case went to the Court of Appeals of Indiana.

The possibility that the whole trial, verdict, and sentencing could be reversed brought on more tension.

Though Angie went, I didn't go because the family support was not as critical this time around. I'd also settled things in my mind that whatever was to be would be. And I didn't want to reopen that deep wound.

WNDU News reported that her new attorney said the jury should not have seen certain photos of Kirk during the trial.

Really? So hiding evidence is appropriate because a person might get convicted for what they did?

The appeal also suggested that another child hitting Kirk could also have led to his death.

Seriously? Another toddler hitting him so hard as to inflict significant injury to brain, optic nerves, and both retinas? Maybe the son of King Kong.

WNDU also reported that the babysitter asserted her sentence was inappropriate because, given that she was sixty years old, serving her sentence meant she would "most likely die in prison." She also argued that numerous letters and other evidence demonstrated her good character. "But the babysitter disregarded the fact that she had a prior conviction for neglect of a dependent and that her battery of a child [Kirk] occurred while she was in a position of trust over him."

The court denied her appeal.

And at the penitentiary she would stay for thirty years. Or at least most of it, as the system goes.

Finally.

But then she appealed again.

That failed.

Finally.

Then she appealed a third time. And this time she was down to a court-appointed attorney who said her case had no merit, and he walked away from it.

Now finally for real.

This dragged-out horrible drama was all over. I now regained my ability to breath in a new way.

And to this day the babysitter does not admit to what she did.

CHAPTER 10

Darkness to Light

WHAT IS THERE TO say in the aftermath of all that happened? A lot, as I've discovered.

We're all one phone call from our knees.[4] We may live in ways that appear confident, even invulnerable, but some things can still crush us, and we're all more fragile that we like to admit.

We also hide our pain in so many places that it seems it all can fragment into pieces.[5] Some pieces get exposed, and we deal with them in time. Others can be so hidden that we ourselves don't see them, and we may go on in pain, not really knowing why.

When the tears flow, it's as if the heart is bleeding, and when that pain of the heart reaches the eyes, it turns to water. Smiles help, but they aren't enough to clear the tears. And keeping ourselves busy only distracts us. Sometimes when our heart empties itself through tears, we feel better afterward. But sometimes, when the emptying

---

4 Mat Kearney, "Closer To Love" on *Closer To Love*. Aware/Columbia, 2009.

5 Stars Go Dim, "You Are Loved" on *You Are Loved*, Fervent Records/Word, 2015.

goes deep enough, it leaves a huge void that even the greatest of memories can only slightly begin to fill. Recovery, back to what we once called "normal," can seem like an insurmountable task.

What then can fill an empty and broken heart?

Many will say love. Love heals and fills a heart. But not any love. An emptied, broken heart needs more than emotional love—or any kind of human love. It needs it's Creator, the One who created the heart in the first place.

The connection to all that is called *faith*. The connection of my faith to the only source that could restore and fill my heart is what I found during the trial. I knew of, and experienced, nothing else that could get me through.

Darkness is always with us in our emptiness and brokenness. It is God's love that provides light. His love is never ending, and all we ultimately need is his love.

If we could only see through God's eyes.[6] Though we cannot see through his eyes, at least in the light he shines on us, we can begin seeing the way he sees.

I think about His sending his Son, knowing full well—even intending—that he would be crucified. This changes how we understand what God allows to happen in our lives. And it changes how we respond to what happens, particularly the bad things. We may begin to see that God is less concerned about how happy we are than he is about our being connected to him in a life of true and deep faith.

---

6 Brandon Heath, "Give Me Yours Eyes" on *What If We*, Reunion Records, 2008.

•

We now see Kirk only in our memories and in picture frames. I want to see him grow up as my children grew up. But I can't. Yet in the light of God's love, I start to see differently.

How selfish I have grown to feel when I want life with Kirk. The world is full of people who have lost far more than my family and I have—people who endure suffering, people who endure injustice.

As the Book of Ecclesiastes says, "There is a time for everything, and a season for every activity under heaven" (3:1). I found that there is a time to fight, and we did that through Kirk's Law, the mistrial, and the trial. And if anything in this tragedy was won, it was protection for other innocents and justice under the law.

Now is the time to let go. The best word for that is *forgiveness*. Why would I, or anyone else ever want to do that? Because I've seen that without forgiveness, we go down a dark and painful path. It's no surprise that God calls us to forgive.

I find that forgiving takes more strength than not forgiving. I might even go so far as to say that not forgiving—being bitter—is a default, easy reaction that exhibits weakness. Forgiving the unforgivable requires strength and a kind of selflessness—exactly what we experience through God's love.

Forgiving sets us free from our own bitterness that otherwise subtly poisons our souls and imprisons our emotions. It can be hard, so hard, to do. But again, that's where faith comes in. That's where we receive the ways that God enables us to become a new kind of person with a heart that heals and fills with his love and strengthens us to do what we otherwise could not do.

This leads me in a new way to the babysitter.

The babysitter herself is a wife, mother, and grandmother. Did she intend for this to happen? I've asked God this question, but he hasn't answered me yet. I doubt she purposely tried to end Kirk's life. There was never any identifiable motive for that. But it was abundantly clear that she had previously hit him, and others, with grievously excessive force far too many times. And she had always gotten away with it—with the one exception of a plea-bargained misdemeanor. And that apparently wasn't enough to get her attention. Maybe she lost touch with how hard she was hitting. Maybe she acted out of embedded, unforgiving pain and anger at being hit when she herself was a child. Maybe that's the example she was raised with, and she thoughtlessly continued the abuse. Maybe, for some psychological reason rooted in her past, she had no tolerance for anyone, even a toddler, who stepped beyond the bounds of her expectations. Maybe her discipline was closer to retribution. And maybe she did not consider or realize or even care how much a toddler might get injured, or much worse, lose their life. If any combination of these are true, I can see how, even at her sentencing, she was blindly self-absorbed enough to claim innocence.

My question finds no answer except in my own thoughts. But I will leave everything where it belongs—with God. When I do so, I have peace. And I have his love.

Forgiveness never means saying a wrongful act was okay. Wrongful acts are never okay. Forgiveness means letting go of the vengeful desire for retribution. The babysitter received her sentence. I would only imprison myself by imagining I could keep her in a prison of my own unforgiveness.

Forgiveness cannot bring back what was lost. But it can restore other things like our relationships, our joy, and our peace of mind. And it can open the way to new and good things that have not yet been.

How deep into one's soul can a person reach for forgiveness? I don't know. But I do know that God has enabled me—and every other person I know who is willing—to reach as far down as needed and to forgive.

Trusting God enables me and countless others with their own stories to forgive what we otherwise could not.

•

I believe that I will never fully understand why Kirk was taken from us. I probably could never fully express my devastated and hopeless feeling of knowing that Kirk would not be with us beyond his nineteen short months. I grieve every time I think about the brevity of his time with us. It's hard to imagine how full of life he was, growing up a young little human, ornery and full of energy. How impossible for me to dream in my worst nightmare that Kirk would not grow into an even more mischievous teenager and emerge into manhood.

To this day I try to hide my tear-stained eyes in hopes I won't be portrayed as a selfish grandfather, still grieving my and my family's loss.

What then about other children who are victims of caregivers? Or countless more who are victims of domestic abuse? How many children grieve inside, unable to express it? Every single one of us has a story of someone grieving. Every story can be devastating in its own way.

And what of children around the world who are victims of war, starvation, child labor, and sex trafficking? The horrors only compound.

The grief of it all is so great as to defy our imagination. And only the heart of God is big enough to absorb it, make any sense of it, and bring redemption.

You may be hurting from your own loss. And God's heart is the only thing that can fully and adequately embrace and absorb your grief or pain.

•

I believe that to fully comprehend and understand why loved ones are taken from us, we must first come to the realization that our loved ones are *given* to us.

That's nice in theory, but then we might ask: Why is it that a babysitter—or anyone else—can take something so precious? This kind of question by itself will drag us back to the conundrum of no good answer that in turn lands us back into bitterness. Adopting the idea that people and things can take loved ones from us can easily plunge us into the bottomless frustration of indignation that never finds an adequate answer. Unchecked, this way of thinking can consume and eventually destroy us—if not outright, then in countless ways that tear at our souls.

I realized through my growing faith in, and understanding of, God, that there is only one source of everything given to us—and taken from us. I took for granted every hour of every day the blessings that God has given. I assumed it all without gratefulness. Instead I only focused on what was taken from me. How unfair is this? How unbalanced is this? In the big picture, a lot.

I've come to understand and experience that ultimately only God gives, and only God takes away.

•

Everyone grieves differently for the loss of a loved one. But one way of thinking we all need to enter is *acceptance*. Acceptance, or lack of it, forms a major part of how we handle that grieving process. If we come to understand that God gives and God takes away, we will be able to accept the results, no matter how bitter they feel at present.

The passing of my loved ones, up until Kirk, I accepted as a part of life. We all have to die sometime. But a child? I could have been so angry with God for allowing Kirk to be taken from us. But if God so chooses or allows something to happen that sends his child home—do we have the authority to blame him? And can we expect that the world, which has largely turned away from God, will change and be nice to each of us?

God blessed me with my mother for twenty-six years. He blessed me knowing my friend Rick for six years. Blessed me with three wonderful sons and a stepdaughter, my wife, two sisters, and four brothers. Many aunts and uncles, cousins, and four grandchildren. All were given to me. All could be taken.

What we choose to accept, and what we focus on, determines everything that follows when we enter a time of loss.

My imagination of life with Kirk—what might have been—is at the feet of God. For anyone in a situation of loss, imagination that fills the emptiness of that loss is natural. If kept in a bitter heart, it will eat away one's soul; if placed at the feet of God, it can bring a semblance of serenity that can only be found when humbly choosing an attitude of faith.

Can I find praise for God in this storm?*[7] I do not praise God *for* the storm. I praise God for his presence *in* the storm. I choose to trust and praise God in the midst of tragedy—as we all must choose one way or the other.

I now realize that through the entire time of my grief, the Holy Spirit was working within me, not only to get through the loss but also to start to see as God sees.

---

7 Casting Crowns, "Praise You in this Storm," on *Lifesong*. Reunion Records, 2005.

CHAPTER 11

Stumbling Toward Hope

THINKING BACK ON WHY I would ever have gotten myself into the Jesus thing, I wondered how that works in the lives of other people. No one lays their head down on their pillow at night and says, "Tomorrow I'm going to wake up as a Christian."

So what moves inside any of us to generate the desire, or need, to move in this direction? Did we previously lack direction for our life? Were we going down the wrong path?

Perhaps every person who makes a decision of faith does so for reasons that are similar to those of other people, yet played out in unique ways to oneself. We're all similar to, yet different from, others. And most of us who decide to become followers of Christ—in the genuine sense and not just warming a seat on Sunday morning—do so for a number of reasons or for a history of successive reasons. Like mine.

My life started well enough, but through a long series of situations and decisions, I spun myself out of control. The events and their consequences ended up controlling. And they were chaotic to where I had no direction left. I was lost. And no matter what I did, I only felt more lost.

My path was of course started by my parents, and having brothers and sisters, I naturally followed some of their paths. Neighborhood and school friends led me down paths of forever-good memories and some not-so-good paths. I'm not sure when I decided to make my own decisions for my life's path. It seems we strive for independence our whole lives. That striving can lead in good directions, but all too easily the directions can slip into bad.

My career path started at age twelve, shining shoes at Knoop's Barber Shop. I thought I would like to become a barber. Then at fourteen I moved upstairs from the barber shop to Breading's Cigar Store, a local hangout for men to play dominoes, drink coffee, and grab breakfast, lunch, or dinner. Since my education level rose no higher than a high school diploma, I often considered my five years at Breading's to be my formal education. I thought I'd like to go into the restaurant business.

After I graduated from high school, a Breading's client offered me a job to head up the receiving department of Kline's Department Store. Still working evenings at Breading's, I thought I'd like to someday head up a retail department at Kline's. I made a few good friends there and dated the store manger's daughter. Both of us were too shy to even kiss.

What I wanted was to get married and have a family, and do it right. But instead I made one bad decision after another. And in the end I produced terrible consequences.

One day the assistant manager and the cosmetic department manager invited another guy and me to have drinks at the local hangout. Then it became a regular pattern. One night we ended up at another co-worker's house. Not good. Hormones and sexual desires are good for procreation, but not for ending up alone with the assistant manager in a bedroom. Alcohol ended my shyness, and from there it just got worse.

My whole life felt broken in every way. My path was not only broken but also going in a direction I could not have fathomed and am deeply ashamed of. I couldn't imagine ever finding a good relationship because I messed this one up so badly. I figured I'd just be single the rest of my life.

I felt ruined and lost.

•

Two very different deaths deeply impacted me and changed the direction of my life in ways that spun it toward the next event.

My best friend from high school, Rick, moved to South Carolina. I visited him a couple of times, and during what would be my final visit with Rick in South Carolina, the great time we were having together got cut short. Rick drove a forklift for the same company that his stepfather had forked for. Rick was catching up on his duties of stacking loads with his forklift. In his haste to catch up, he lifted a load high up and turned to place it on a shelf. As he turned, the forklift tipped forward and Rick was thrown off. His head hit the concrete floor and he lost his life. I was more saddened for his mother's loss than mine.

It was so sudden. And it left me feeling lost and broken.

My mother was an amazing person who raised five children and helped rear two stepchildren. She was a respected elementary school teacher for twenty years. She died of cancer when she was only fifty-one years old. I was more saddened for my father's loss than my own, especially because he had lost his first wife to leukemia. Yet I held no remorse against God for calling my mother to heaven.

Her passing was gradual and expected. I accepted her death as a natural part of life, and I saw the hurt and loss in the people left in the wake of her passing.

Yet despite my acceptance, I felt even more broken and lost.

I was also too hurt, confused, and dysfunctional to even think of having a serious relationship.

Then, after a few more miserable years, I met a woman in a bar. She became my first wife. Together, besides her daughter, we had Chad, Cody, and later Alex. Eventually things went bad, and the marriage ended.

There was a woman I knew before I had even met my first wife, and for awkward reasons, along with our youth, we were forced to go our separate ways. We met again and both knew that we each wanted to—and could successfully—spend the rest of our lives together. A few years after my divorce, Karrie and I wedded. We've had a good marriage since and will continue.

I love this woman, my wife, though we have not lived our lives as Christians by any means. After I started attending church, she has occasionally gone with me. And I trust her in God's hands that God will lead her on her own spiritual journey toward hope.

•

My experiences until Kirk's death were not enough to turn my life around. I just bumbled through things toward the next life event or mess—whatever that might be—spinning in one direction then bumping and spinning into another direction.

When Kirk died, his death and loss became more intensely personal than I had ever before experienced. His childhood innocence and all that happened cut deep and hard into my whole being. I could not accept his death the way I had accepted Rick's and Mother's deaths, or the way I had accepted so many other things, as I just keep bumping and spinning through life.

Because Kirk's death should never have happened, not by chance, not by disease, and not by inevitability—and because there was so much wrong about it that it was morally repugnant to me—I determined I would not bump and spin into yet another lost direction. I would commit to this direction no matter what happened. At this point in my aimless life I had to.

Feeling shaken to my core, I can see how I was forced to realize that the only way I could get through this was to turn to something or someone greater than myself. And the greatest one I could turn to was God. And it became clear to me that that God intentionally incarnated himself as a person, Jesus Christ, and walked on this earth.

Blessed is anyone who finally feels broken enough to stop bumbling, bumping, and spinning through life, to get shaken to their core, and decisively open their eyes to the deep need of their soul in the face of eternity.

Looking back I cannot avoid saying that it was the Holy Spirit's prompting me to recognize the amazing gift God had given humanity and was inviting me to be a part. If he can do it for me, he can do it for anyone.

My attitude has radically changed, particularly in my acceptance of other people and in my attitude about work. I'm even a better, kinder driver than I used to be. At work I'm known as "the guy who smiles all the time." I'm asked things like, "What's your secret?" Or, "Why do you come to work with a smile every day?" I have relationship with my Creator, and I am learning his perspective on life. This life is a sliver of time compared to eternity. And I know what's ahead of me, my earthly future is always with God, and so is my eternity.

•

I have continually found inexplicable guidance in every aspect of my life. This guidance has helped me in hard situations at work, with family, with money, relationships, and seemingly everything in my life. There is no other explanation for this other than the Spirit of God being alive and active in my life. It is truly amazing. And all I can say about why I receive all this is, first, that I know God loves me—not because of who I am but because of who he is.[8] And second, I've been lost and broken so much for so long that I've grown humbled and open to receiving what God has for me. I am sure he has more for most of us than we realize or have had the open heart and mind to receive.

If I ever had any doubt about God in my life, it's long gone now. And I still experience God's continual guidance through the presence of his Spirit in me—a gift that enables me to see past pain.

---

8 Casting Crowns, "Who Am I," on *Casting Crowns*. Reunion Records, 2003.

CHAPTER 12

Seeing Past the Pain

AFTER A TRAGEDY—OR MAYBE at any time during any week—how far out of reach can our God be? I believe he is as far away as we want him to be. I won't judge, but when I look around, it seems a lot of people want him to stay far away from the lives they choose to live. As we choose to be near God, he is as close as we want him to be. As we push him away, away from us he will go.

Regardless of what life brings our way, the degree of his presence in our lives is up to us. I believe that this is his intent. Our part is to acknowledge and embrace his presence that's already there.

This never means there won't be pain. Pain is where we often meet God.

In too many countries around the world, a child living only nineteen months—or less—is tragically common. My story is one of millions, many of them worse.

Poor hygiene, malnutrition, disease, war, and abuse kill far too many kids who never get the chance to live out their lives. Too many mothers and fathers and grandparents and families weep and ache.

And almost no one sees or hears them because poverty or oppression make them almost invisible.

But God sees them. And I suspect that God weeps with them. In the eyes of God, those lost children are every bit as valued and loved as Kirk.

And what about the child, spouse, sibling, or friend you love? They are just as valuable.

The things I've discovered, the feelings about them, and the lessons learned are universal. Each of us writes our own story. How will you write yours?

•

When we look past the pain, from where does our healing come? Some sickness can be healed by doctors and by medication. But when our soul is torn apart, from where does that healing come? I believe there is only one source that could even come close to healing a hurting soul. As I have experienced, I am now convinced, we must turn to the maker of heaven and earth. One can ask, "Why would he create us and make us endure pain?" Or, "Why is there evil in this world?"

We need to be willing—because only then are we able—to look beyond ourselves. Even when answers are elusive, when we look beyond our personal issues, we will see, feel, and grow in ways that carry us through the pain.

Without darkness, would we be able to see the light? And without experiencing sadness, would we truly know happiness? And without hardship, would we ever see our need for God? The Bible, for example, is full of stories where God lets his people suffer in hopes that they'll turn to him.

I believe he has a plan for each of us. I trust in his ways,[9] no matter how painful life may be at times. Does believing this lessen the pain? No, but it does something better. The pain is real, but trusting God makes the pain flow through me and out of me so that it doesn't consume me. God absorbs the pain and gives me his love and peace in return.

So who is the great healer? Jesus Christ, the incarnation of God who came to earth and healed sickness. It was he who absorbed the penalty for our sin—the worst kind of sickness of soul—on the cross. And he still does it through his Spirit, the Holy Spirit, who lives in all who believe.

I'll always be human, and I'll always have heroes—especially the ones God gives me as part of my life's healing. Larry and Will are heroes of my faith. Vicki is my hero for prosecuting Kirk's case with passion and caring. Senator Carlin Yoder is my hero for sponsoring Kirk's law. Then governor Mike Pence is my hero for signing Kirk's law with so much compassion for our family.

I don't want to take anything away from heroes in my life, but the one and only true hero is Jesus Christ, our Lord and Savior. How ironic it is to think that the villainous babysitter I described would awaken the Holy Spirit within me. God does in fact work in mysterious ways. I confess I fall short of the glory of God every single day. But I know his love is unconditional for all of us—heroes and villains alike.

---

9 Lauren Daigle, "Trust in You," on *How Can It Be*. Centricity Music, 2015.

•

Though most people seem to seek a high status, I've come to see that God cuts through all that to see us as equals. The more important difference is where people are in their faith. I approach this very cautiously. Religion and politics are touchy subjects at places of business and in public. Yet I consistently observe that people who believe in God tend to have a happy presence. I am intrigued by how bright their view on the world is.[10] I'm not saying these believers don't have negative views about some things, just that they have a more joyful or positive demeanor and outlook that others don't exhibit so much.

And me too. Since I've been following Christ and growing in faith, I've noticed a change in my attitude towards people. I've gained an indescribable kind of tolerance for people, and more empathy towards them. Like those I observe, my own world is made brighter by my belief. I believe the future is bright, so bright, after life in this world. How bright is your world?

Our beliefs define us in huge, life-encompassing ways. Some are subtle, others overt. My experience has shown me that being without faith, not only spiritual faith, but any faith at all, is a terrible way to go through life. Faith adds that brightness to our lives that only comes when we allow God's love to shine through.

The most common way to observe or express this is through smiles. A smile is a window to the soul. I believe common, earthly-attained smiles are just on our face's surface. Those smiles that come from the depths of our soul, our core, are different. A smile rises from thoughts of my family, my children, and of my friends.

10 Brandon Heath, "The Light In Me," on *Leaving Eden*. Reunion Records, 2011.

Experiences and events generate surface smiles; being with family and friends during those experiences and events, as well as deeply appreciating things in life, generates core smiles. I believe God is so passionate about us that everyone is sent the same gifts. Core smiles are also heaven-sent from God, our heavenly Father. The Bible calls them "joy in the Lord."

So beyond our own appreciations, this gift of joy in the midst of sadness comes from God, and we must make certain to receive it. And we do so by believing in Him and receiving Jesus Christ as our personal Savior and sovereign Lord, whom we can trust.

The differences between people come in how we respond to God's gifts. Let me use my friend Larry as an example. When he smiles, I see the glean in his eyes and can tell he has received and embraced his core smile; his soul and spirit seem to be smiling along with him. It's the same with my friend Will in the joy he has when sharing his love for Jesus; it radiates from him through his smile.

I enjoy smiling at people, and most smile back. I feel sad when they don't. I also notice the difference in their smiles. Some seem to be polite return smiles. Others hold more "value," like the ones who are sharing their core smile. I still appreciate the polite smiles. Maybe those people are more reserved or are going through something at the time. But when I recognize what I perceive to be a core smile, I warm up to that person's bright window to their soul. Find your core smile. Be thankful for it and show it. It adds face value!

Moving from our face to our hands, as toddlers we are taught fine motor skills to hold on to things with our hands. We use our hands to hold things, to color with crayons and then to write with pencils and pens. We grow to hold our loved ones with our hands. And if we can just wrap our hands around a problem, we expect to solve it. Going a step further, I have experienced that if we take hold, or take ownership, of our problems rather than lay blame, and then place them in the hands of the One who can solve all our problems, by prayer and faith, it lessens the burden.

•

As I reflect back on my life, I admit that so many hardships would have been easier and quicker to work through or overcome if I had thought and acted differently by believing, praying, and trusting the process and the outcome to our Creator, our God. I believe his grace knows no boundaries. How much might your quality of life improve if you did the same?

I think about a Father's sending his only Son to be crucified. How much faith it took for Jesus knowing he would be put to a horrible death. And even more faith to rise from the grave. Just thinking about it, my problems seem insignificant. The amount of trust and faith Jesus had, the same power, I believe lives in all of us.[11] What our Savior did for us is truly amazing.

I used to get hung up on the meaning of why we are here on earth. Why didn't God just create us as spirit beings who stay in heaven in the first place? Why does humanity have to go through all the pain and hassles of this world? I've seen through my life that this life teaches us, even forces us, to grow in character and integrity. And this is why we're here.

Since coming to faith, this realization has risen to a whole new level. Truth be told, I still go back and ask myself why I'm here on

---

11 Jeremy Camp, "Same Power," on *I Will Follow*. Sparrow, 2015.

earth. Yet some questioning about why I'm on earth and what kind of person am I is a good thing because I ask deeper questions about the kind of person I am and the quality and integrity of life I'm living.

I can't fathom the power of our God. How could he create all of this? It is so overwhelming.[12] I don't pretend to understand the creation, but I have found every reason to believe Jesus is "the way, the truth, and the life," and that he is humanity's way to salvation (John 14:6).

There is no way possible I can fully grasp a tragedy like the loss of a child. It would consume me, and I think eventually destroy me, if I tried. This kind of thing consumes, and occasionally destroys, others who carry unfathomable grief. Yet nothing gives me more satisfaction than knowing Kirk is in the hands of Jesus.

Tragedy led me to God. We all have so many possible paths to travel. I went down some of them, and indeed they lead downward, bumping and spinning their way first to personal and then to eternal oblivion. Life after Kirk has shown me the best, and the right, path to follow. In fact, I now accept this as the only path to follow. So I take my hands off and put everything in the hands of our heavenly Father.[13]

---

12 Big Daddy Weave, "Overwhelmed," on *Love Come To Life*. Fervent Records/Word, 2012.

13 Tenth Avenue North, "Control," on *Followers*. Reunion Records, 2016.

•

I encourage you to welcome his presence in your life and experience his glory. His love never fails.[14] He has been the same through all of the ages. And he is still the same for you.

---

14 Newsboys, "Your Love Never Fails," on *God's Not Dead*. InPop Records, 2011.

- End -